WHAT'S NEW?

Recent developments included in this supplement

- Analyzes the difference between Mild Head Injury and Post Concussion Syndrome
- Probes the actual ability of Neuro Psychological tests to predict outcome in Closed Head injuries
- Case review of
    - traumatic epilepsy as a result of head trauma
    - injuries to the neck and associated structures
    - temporomandibular joint injuries (TMJ)
    - personality change as a result of closed head trauma
    - mental or neurological conditions

HEAD TRAUMA CASES
LAW AND MEDICINE
SECOND EDITION
VOLUME 1

1997 Supplement Current through December 26, 1996

by

ARTHUR C. ROBERTS

*****HERE'S WHAT'S NEW INSIDE*****

- Review detailed analyses of the difference between Mild Head Injury and Post Concussion Syndrome, Volume 1, see page 5.
- Take a closer look at the actual ability of Neuro Psychological tests to predict outcome in Closed Head injuries, Volume 1, see page 6.
- Receive valuable case review of:
  - traumatic epilepsy as a result of head trauma
  - injuries to the neck and associated structures
  - temporomandibular joint injuries (TMJ)
  - personality change as a result of closed head trauma
  - mental or neurological conditions
- and more, see page i for details.

Insert in the pocket in the back inside cover of the bound book.

Wiley Law Publications
JOHN WILEY & SONS, INC.
New York • Chichester • Weinheim • Brisbane • Singapore • Toronto

ROBERTS/HEAD TRAUMA 2E 2VST 97S
ISBN 0-471-18463-2

This text is printed on acid-free paper.

Library of Congress Cataloging-in-Publication Data

ISBN 0-471-12182-7 (set)
ISBN 0-471-12298-X (vol. 1)
ISBN 0-471-12299-8 (vol. 2)
ISBN 0-471-18463-2 (supplement)

Printed in the United States of America

10 9 8 7 6 5 4 3 2 1

PREFACE

The reception of *Litigating Head Trauma Cases* has been both satisfying and gratifying. In this new text, *Head Trauma Cases: Law and Medicine,* the two-volume format has demonstrated its utility, not only to the practicing attorney, but to experts working in the field of head trauma, and other professionals and paraprofessionals involved in this exciting and complex field.

At the time of the publication of the first edition of *Litigating Head Trauma Cases,* the topic of closed head injury was in a state of evolution and much that is now quite well established in research and clinical practice was then speculation and consisted of a number of theoretical explanations for clinical observations.

Since the original text, obviously, the field has matured, but the topic of mild head injury and the postconcussion syndrome remains highly charged with controversy. The disorder clearly represents a combination of neurogenic and psychogenic components; the relative predominance of each element depends upon (a) the original biomechanical forces applied to the person's head, (b) the constitutional and personal endowment of the particular person, and (c) the particular orientation of the treating personnel. This latter element is of no small consequence. If a person becomes convinced that he or she has a serious and protracted neurologic disorder, then all sorts of adverse consequences necessarily follow. This results in prolonged disability and, in some cases, a greatly restricted manner of living subsequent to the precipitating event. Conversely, the insistence that all of these symptoms are "in the patient's head" discounts the obvious distress of the individual and places no emphasis on the clear neurogenic components of mild head injury. Again, a thorough-going analysis of the biomechanical forces appears to be the most rational way to determine the severity of the injury.

In that regard, then, the most logical and compelling development is an attempt to quantify these forces. **Chapter 2,** "Biomechanics of Closed Head Injury," has begun to address this issue, but obviously a considerable amount of refinement is necessary to more clearly quantify the forces of acceleration/deceleration and the correlations of these forces with brain tissue impairment. This will constitute the next major project of this author and will be incorporated into the next edition of this text.

In the meantime, we have instituted a series of interesting and, in some cases, provocative trial decisions and settlements involving head injury, in its manifest forms. This text will continue to evolve and refine, it is the aim of the principal author, and the contributing authors, to provide a definitive text for both clinician and attorney which is in all respects contemporaneous as to both the medical and legal aspects of this complicated and challenging field.

Colorado Springs, Colorado
March 1997

ARTHUR C. ROBERTS

NEW IN THIS SUPPLEMENT

Note to the Reader: Materials that appear only in the supplement and not in the main volume are listed below.

MEDICAL MALPRACTICE TITLES FROM WILEY LAW PUBLICATIONS

ATTORNEY'S GUIDE TO ONCOLOGY CASES
Melvin A. Shiffman and Pierre V. Haig

BASES OF LIABILITY
Michael D. McCafferty and Steven M. Meyer

DENTAL MALPRACTICE: LEGAL AND MEDICAL HANDBOOK (THIRD EDITION)
Norman L. Schafler

EMERGENCY MEDICINE MALPRACTICE (SECOND EDITION)
Mikel A. Rothenberg

HANDLING CARDIOLOGY AND CARDIOVASCULAR SURGERY CASES
James B. Rosenblum and Charles L. Curry

HANDLING GENERAL SURGERY CASES
Melvin A. Shiffman

HANDLING INTERNAL MEDICINE CASES
Alvin Lee Block

HANDLING OPHTHALMOLOGY CASES
Sander Marc Rabin

HANDLING ORTHOPEDIC CASES
William N. Harsha

HANDLING UROLOGY CASES
William J. Morton

LEGAL GUIDE TO PATIENT COMPLIANCE
Raymond A. Ulmer

1996 WILEY MEDICAL MALPRACTICE UPDATE
Wiley Law Editors

OBSTETRIC AND NEONATAL MALPRACTICE: LEGAL AND MEDICAL HANDBOOK (SECOND EDITION)
Michael D. Volk

PHARMACY LAW
David B. Brushwood

PLASTIC SURGERY MALPRACTICE AND DAMAGES
Jeffrey D. Robertson and William T. Keavy

PSYCHIATRIC CARE
Joseph T. Smith

THE RIGHT TO DIE (SECOND EDITION)
Alan Meisel

CHAPTER 3

CLOSED HEAD INJURY SYNDROME IN ADULTS

§ 3.40 Verdicts and Settlements (New)

The following cases involve traumatic epilepsy as a result of head trauma:

In *Higgins v. Lufi,* 353 N.W.2d 150 (Minn. App. 1984), an action brought against babysitters for allowing a child to fall into a stairwell, resulting in a skull fracture causing epilepsy, the jury awarded $750,000 to the child and $81,500 to her parents, and the judgment based on these awards was affirmed. The court noted, apparently on the basis of expert testimony at trial, that the child, who was three years old at the time of the injury and in kindergarten at the time of the trial, would probably require daily medication to suppress seizures for the rest of her life, and had a 75 percent chance of developing major motor epilepsy as a child.

A damage award on behalf of a mentally retarded boy who was allegedly struck on the head by a baseball thrown by a teacher was upheld (and increased) despite the fact that the boy's first epileptic episode occurred nearly two and one-half years after the accident. It was for the jury to decide whether the boy's epilepsy was traumatically induced or whether it was caused by a preexisting condition that had caused a proliferation of cranial bony and soft tissue tumors. *Figliomeni v. Board of Education,* 38 N.Y.2d 178, 379 N.Y.S.2d 45, 341 N.E.2d 557 (1975) (upholding increase of award of $125,000 to $175,000).

An industrial commission claimant failed to sustain his burden of proof that there was a causal relationship between his work-related automobile accident, in which he suffered a laceration on his forehead, and the convulsive epileptic disorders that developed seven months later. The only expert testimony in this regard was that of a neurosurgeon who stated the claimant had "an extremely large complicated bilateral cerebral vascular malformation" which had probably been in development throughout claimant's life and rendered him "unusually susceptible to a head injury." The neurosurgeon also testified that there was a possibility that the accident aggravated the problem. *Friesner v. Industrial Comm.,* 14 Ariz. App. 232, 482 P.2d 481 (1971).

A 55-year-old chief of pharmacy of the State Department of Social Services, who was a hotel guest attending a convention, was abducted from his hotel room, and was severely beaten and left unconscious on the street, was awarded $400,000, by remittitur, for permanent damage to the brain; the consequences were continuing headaches, traumatic neurosis, and epilepsy which could be controlled only by a drug that caused side effects. *Margreiter v. New Hotel Monteleone, Inc.,* 640 F.2d 508 (5th Cir. 1981).

In *Garlepied v. Mechanical Constr., Inc.,* 540 So. 2d 616 (La. App. 5th 1989), the court upheld the denial of a workers compensation claim, finding that there was insufficient evidence to show that the claimant's epileptic seizures were caused by an accident in which the claimant was struck by a falling ladder. Although the claimant alleged that he complained of headache when he sought treatment for a separated shoulder caused by the accident, the doctors who examined the claimant did not testify that he had suffered a head injury or complained of a headache. A neurologist who examined the claimant two years after the accident testified that the claimant's seizures were caused by a head injury, but there was no evidence to link the head injury to the ladder accident.

In *Good Shepherd Workshop v. Workmen's Compensation Appeal Bd.* (Caffrey), 124 Pa. Comm. 262, 555 A.2d 1374 (1989), a retarded adult's award of benefits for an epileptic condition was upheld. The court found that there was sufficient evidence that the epilepsy was a result of a fall at work in which the claimant struck her head on the floor, lost consciousness, stopped breathing, turned blue, and required mouth-to-mouth resuscitation. Although the claimant had cerebral damage from a non-specific prenatal injury, a medical expert testified that it was unlikely that the fall was the result of an epileptic seizure, since the sudden onset of incapacitating seizures at the claimant's age, without any previous history of seizures, did not fit any of the three medically recognized categories of epilepsy resulting from prenatal injury. The expert also testified that the "focal" seizures that the claimant experienced within an hour of the fall at work were consistent with localized injury to the brain such as would be caused by the trauma of a head injury, and would be completely inconsistent with the onset of epilepsy resulting from prenatal injury. The referee rejected testimony by the employer's expert that, in his opinion, the claimant's seizures were not caused by her head injury at work.

The jury awarded plaintiff $800,000 for serious injuries she sustained in an automobile accident. On appeal, defendant contended the trial court erred in overruling defendant's objection to a portion of the final argument by plaintiff's counsel in which counsel referred to a "potential" for epilepsy and meningitis as factors to be considered in assessing damages. The court agreed with defendant and remanded the case for a new trial. The court reasoned that damages cannot be awarded for a possible result of an injury, but only for a result that is reasonably certain to occur. By using the word "potential" counsel in essence informed the jury it could award plaintiff damages for epilepsy and meningitis that might possibly develop later. Quoting extensively from the relevant portions of the transcript, the court concluded that at most the evidence suggested a possibility of future difficulties—it did not establish a reasonable certainty plaintiff would suffer from epilepsy or meningitis in the future. However, on a petition to transfer, the Supreme Court held that the $800,000 award was not excessive and that because defendants had allowed expert testimony regarding plaintiff's potential for epilepsy and meningitis without objection, plaintiff's attorney could properly refer to such testimony in his closing argument when his statements were couched in the exact language the witnesses had used. *Dayton Walther Corp. v. Caldwell,* 389 N.E.2d 723 (Ind. App. 1979).

A neurosurgeon testifying for a 4-year-old child who had suffered a fractured skull and brain contusions testified that a child who had suffered such injuries had 1 chance in 20 of developing seizures at some time in the future, up to 15 or 20 years later. The court held this testimony was properly admitted, stating that the witness was not speculating when he indicated the probability of epileptic seizures based on statistics in his field of expertise. Although the probability of epilepsy was low, it should be weighed by the jury accordingly. If the jury failed to do so, the proper remedy would be an objection to the excessiveness of the verdict. *Schwegel v. Goldberg,* 209 Pa. Super. 280, 228 A.2d 405 (1967).

A damage award on behalf of a four-year-old boy was upheld where, despite disputed interpretations of EEG examinations, the jury could have found that there was a brain injury resulting from the car collision in which the boy was involved which caused "epileptic type activity," and though the condition was controllable by medication and recovery might be expected within four to six years, the condition could also be permanent. *Roth v. Kanchier,* 91 Ill. App. 2d (abstract) 111, 234 N.E.2d 59 (1968).

In an action for damages arising out of a car accident in which a four-year-old girl was injured, the defendant's expert testified that the plaintiff's petit mal epilepsy attacks showed up on EEG tracings as "electronic emanations" that were not necessarily the result of an accident, since such EEG tracings are seen in children who have not been in accidents and who have little overt evidence of seizures. Nevertheless, the court held the jury had the right to believe, from the testimony of the plaintiff's expert, that the EEG tracings indicated that the plaintiff had several kinds of epilepsy, petit mal and grand mal, that her sudden falling asleep constituted epileptic episodes, and that such incidents were caused by the automobile accident. *Bash v. Employers Mut. Liability Ins. Co.,* 38 Wis. 2d 440, 157 N.W.2d 634 (1968).

In an action for personal injuries suffered by the plaintiff when one of the wheels of his pickup truck fell off and the ensuing jolt left him unconscious, the evidence was sufficient to establish the necessary causal relationship between the accident and a reoccurrence of the plaintiff's previous epilepsy, where there was testimony by a physician that the reoccurrence of the plaintiff's epileptic seizures was more likely than not the result of the injury which the plaintiff suffered in the accident, and where circumstantial evidence showed that the plaintiff's doctor had, prior to the accident, attained such control over the plaintiff's seizures that the plaintiff had not had a grand mal seizure for 16 years nor a petit mal seizure for 8 years, and that as a direct result of the accident he suffered a period of unconsciousness and 2 days later experienced a grand mal seizure and within 5 months began complaining of uncontrollable laughter and incontinence, the symptoms of his petit mal seizures. *Leak v. United States Rubber Co.,* 9 Wash. App. 98, 511 P.2d 88 (1973).

CHAPTER 4

POSTCONCUSSION SYNDROME

§ 4.2A —Is There a Difference Between "Mild Head Injury" and "Postconcussion Syndrome"? (New)

In § **4.2** it is stated "Postconcussion Syndrome (PCS) may be defined as that injury caused by trauma to the head, accompanied by a transient loss of consciousness (less than 20 minutes) and/or a significant degree of mental confusion, that has an initial Glasgow Coma Scale (GCS) score of 13 to 15." That statement was made in earlier editions of this text and I should like to emphasize that it is important to modify that statement. Over time there has evolved a greater precision in nomenclature in discussions of traumatic brain injury. The postconcussion syndrome is called "postconcussional disorder" in the Diagnostic and Statistical Manual (1994) of the American Psychiatric Association (DSM-IV) which is based upon the recommendations of Brown et al. S. Brown, "Post Concussional Disorder: Time to Acknowledge a Common Source of Neurobehavioral Morbidity," 6 *J. Neuropsychiatry Clin. Neurosci.* 15–22 (1994). It includes the proposed criteria for making this diagnosis. By the DSM-IV criteria, a history of head injury is, by definition, the threshold consideration. To qualify for this diagnosis, current symptoms should include deficits in recall and/or concentration (cognitive difficulties). An excellent review article reports that a major source of confusion in the literature on head injury is related to the failure to differentiate between the cognitive consequences of traumatic brain injury and those of postconcussion syndrome. "Since PCS can occur in the absence of TBI, and are inversely related to the severity of injury, they clearly result from substantially different factors." The authors state that the failure to differentiate PCS from TBI "has resulted in much of the confusion regarding when recovery from minor head injury occurs." M. Kibby et al., "Minor Head Injury: Attempts at Clarifying the Confusion," 10(3) *Brain Injury* 159–186 (1996). The authors define *minor head injury* as a term including individuals who have suffered from traumatic brain injury (TBI) in a continuum from mild to moderate severity. In the earlier literature on head injury, "mild" and "minor" head injury were considered equivalent. In my opinion, both terms underplay the seriousness of the disorder that characterizes the recovery in many individuals.

Regardless, it is clear that there is considerable confusion among the terms used in this field. Some authorities state that the postconcussion syndrome is essentially confined to cognitive symptoms. The DSM-IV criteria include a number of other symptoms that could easily be ascribed to either psychological (emotional or personality) variables or to the effects of parenchymal damage. All or most of these symptoms are found following mild head injury, at least transiently, but it is often a fact, the reasons for which are poorly understood, that these symptoms are less frequently found in those who recover from more severe head injuries.

Out of this welter of confused nomenclature, one fact remains constant: the degree of brain tissue damage is highly correlated with increase in the rate of change of velocity, usually deceleration, particularly in the case of motor vehicle accidents. This is not to say that outcome and subsequent disability is fully related to this variable, because, as has been frequently stated, factors such as expectancy, secondary gain, involvement in litigation, etc., may play a powerful role in subsequent recovery.

§ 4.16A —Do Neuropsychological Test Scores Accurately Parallel Functional Abilities and Are They Predictive of Outcome in Closed Head Injury? (New)

In this text there are frequent references to both the utility and the inherent limitations of neuropsychological testing in assessing the cognitive impairment deriving from a mild head injury. As has been noted frequently throughout the text, factors other than the undoubted parenchymal damage that is sustained in many mild head injuries should be factored into analyzing the cognitive deficits that are presumed to be an inherent part of the symptom complex. Conscientious neuropsychologists have always been aware of many of the inherent limitations of standard test batteries. Both over- and under-interpretation of test data can lead to unfortunate consequences in a head-injured individual's rehabilitation when neuropsychological testing becomes a core element in determining prognosis.

Problems of under-diagnosis, in my opinion, generally derive from the inadequacy of neuropsychological testing in assessing damage in those areas of the brain that are most frequently impacted by acceleration-deceleration induced head injury—that is, the under-surface of the frontal lobes. Without going into technical detail regarding what tests are either deficient or useful in detecting lesions in this area, suffice it to say that they are generally considered to be inadequate by neuroscientists. In fact, various types of "organic" personality deficits may characterize this syndrome, and may themselves be the major cause of cognitive deficit. Personality deficits are, perhaps, inherently unquantifiable. Thus, the best analysis of the impact of these trauma-induced personality changes derives from the observations of significant others, including employers and co-workers. Family members often have the inherent and understandable tendency to ascribe changes in an individual to a particular event, such as a motor vehicle accident. This problem is, of course, compounded by the process of litigation. (This latter statement is not meant to imply that such persons are always malingering their disorders, but, as has been mentioned in this text, that "expectation as etiology" is a factor always present. See **§ 4.23.**) The authors of an intriguing paper noted "patients consistently underestimated the pre-morbid prevalence of these (postconcussion) symptoms compared with the base rate in controls. Symptom expectations appear to share as much variance with the Post Concussion Syndrome as head injury itself." W. Millenberg et al., "Symptoms Following Mild Head Injury: Expectation as Etiology," 55 *J. Neurology, Neurosurgery and Psychiatry* 200–204 (1992). Even when it is abundantly clear, from an analysis of the individual's performance at work, at school, and in other aspects of everyday functioning, cognitive impairment can seriously impact such persons' lives, particularly when combined with the frequently-encountered personality change and affective disturbance that characterize recovery from head injury. It would be more useful to place greater emphasis on these observable factors than in specific test scores and labels. As a matter of fact, it is not entirely clear as to what specific everyday cognitive functioning neuropsychological tests measure. In an editorial response to an article in the journal cited immediately above, Brick Johnstone commented that the "inappropriate labeling of tests leads to inappropriate interpretations." This fact represents what is called a "construct validity" of the tests employed by neuropsychologists. Commonly used neuropsychological tests have not been adequately demonstrated to have complete construct validity.

In summary, it appears to this author, from a careful analysis of literally hundreds of papers published on the topic, and from extensive consultation and contact with clinical neuropsychologists, that there is, generally, an over-emphasis on neuropsychological test scores as predictors of global outcome. Variables other than neuropsychological test scores, including the individual's response to the accident, his or her socio-economic and cultural status, and a host of factors variously described as constituting "secondary gain" are, in my opinion, far more predictive of outcome than are neuropsychological test scores taken in isolation from such variables. I think it is generally true that responsible neuropsychologists would agree with this statement. These remarks apply, primarily, to neuropsychological testing in mild head injury characterized by the so-called "postconcussion syndrome." More severe and clear-cut cognitive deficits, reflected in global problems with motor performance, for example, are not difficult to replicate by certain standardized neuropsychological tests. However, the problem is generally obvious from an analysis of the individual's day-to-day functioning. It may be simply reinforcing the obvious to confirm these deficits through neuropsychological testing.

§ 4.24 Verdicts and Settlements (New)

The following miscellaneous cases involve injuries as a result of head trauma:

Evidence established that an infant plaintiff suffered permanent brain injury in a fall, although the examining neurologist found no evidence of any lasting structural or behavioral change in the infant's brain and opined that the infant had made a full recovery, where the psychologist and the psychiatrist testified that the infant demonstrated a personality disorder and a learning disability, that he would probably never graduate from high school, and that his prognosis for recovery was poor because brain tissue is irreparable and the brain damage was permanent. *Hernandez v. New York,* 156 App. Div. 2d 641, 549 N.Y.S.2d 139 (1989).

In a personal injury action arising from an automobile accident, substantial evidence existed to establish medical causation, where the clinical neuropsychologist and the psychiatrist both testified that, based upon evaluation of the injured party and discussions with his family, the head trauma sustained in the accident created a brain trauma which caused a temporal lobe disorder resulting in an organic brain syndrome, and testimony of members of the family established the extreme mood swings typical of the condition and their origin after the auto accident. *Patrick v. Alphin,* 825 S.W.2d 11 (Mo. App. 1992).

An award of $125,000 to a 76-year-old painter who fell from a stepladder and struck his head was held not excessive, where the evidence showed that after the incident the plaintiff began to suffer from headaches and gradual physical and mental deterioration, that he suffered memory loss and frequently became disoriented, that he became incontinent, and that one month later he was hospitalized and brain surgery was performed for a subdural hematoma, and where although plaintiff's condition had much improved since surgery, he had not recovered the same mental sharpness and vigor as he had before the accident. *Mote v. Montgomery Ward & Co.,* 125 Ill. App. 3d 839, 81 Ill. Dec. 7, 466 N.E.2d 593 (3d Dist. 1984)

An award of $390,000 to a woman injured in an automobile collision was held not excessive, where the evidence showed that she was hospitalized four days with a broken nose, dislodged teeth, contusions to her mouth, dizziness, disorientation, and a concussion, where there was testimony that she suffered a probable basilar skull fracture causing leakage of cerebral spinal fluid with potential for future complications from infection, including meningitis, brain abscess, or other neurological problems, and where there was medical testimony as to significant emotional and psychological damages that plaintiff suffered as a result of her injury. *Davis v. Graviss,* 672 S.W.2d 928 (Ky. 1984).

CHAPTER 6

INJURIES TO THE NECK AND ASSOCIATED STRUCTURES

§ 6.22 Verdicts and Settlements (New)

The following cases involve injuries to the neck and associated structures:

In a workers' compensation claim, notice of a claim for "upper back and shoulder, thoracic strain" was sufficient to include the cervical area so that it was error for the trial court to dismiss a claim for "cervical strain" on the grounds that the worker had not filed a timely claim as required by RC § 4123.84 where the worker had filed a timely claim for upper back strain; in general terms "lumbar" describes the lower back, "thoracic" describes the middle back, and "cervical" the upper back and neck; here a claim was specifically allowed for the upper back, a term which includes the cervical area. *Bishop v. Mayfield,* 65 Ohio App. 3d 544, 584 N.E.2d 1242 (Fayette County 1989).

Award of $10,000 to passenger in automobile that was rear-ended was inadequate; passenger suffered cervical sprain/strain as well as injury that originated in right side of his neck and progressed to his temporomandibular joint. Given inadequate awards for past medical expenses and general damages, total award would be increased to $31,147, which included $5,000 in general damages for cervical sprain/strain and $10,000 in general damages for TMJ dysfunction. *Stoutes v. General Motors Acceptance Corp.,* 598 So. 2d 654 (La. App. 3d 1992).

Motorist could be cross-examined about her settlement of a previous claim involving an identical injury, where the motorist testified that she suffered soft-tissue injuries to her neck and back, and the trial court declared a mistrial when opponent attempted to cross-examine her about treatment of her previous injury after she settled the previous claim; defendant wanted to show that the motorist stopped all treatment after settling the previous claim, and this line of questioning was relevant to determining the credibility of the motorist's testimony regarding her soft tissue injuries in the present accident. *Zenchak v. Kaeufer,* 612 So. 2d 725, 18 W.D. Fla. 423 (Fla. App. 1993).

The evidence was sufficient to establish that the decedent's neck and shoulder pains that troubled her during what would be her final years of life were caused by an automobile accident and not the cancer which claimed her life where (1) she testified at a deposition that such pains did not manifest themselves before the accident and were continuous thereafter, and (2) a physician expressed his opinion that the neck and shoulder pains were caused by the accident. *Gompers v. Finnell,* 35 Mass. App. 91, 616 N.E.2d 490 (1993).

Although a jury award of $85,000 for the plaintiff's pain and suffering due to soft-tissue back injuries sustained in the automobile accident was generous given plaintiff's age and general physical condition, the award was not so excessive as to shock the conscience of the court and require reduction. *Lauria v. New York City Dep't of Environmental Protection,* 152 Misc. 2d 543, 577 N.Y.S.2d 764 (Civ. Ct. 1991).

Jury verdict of $75,000 in personal injury action was excessive, despite fact that plaintiff suffered recurring headaches after sustaining concussion and neck injuries when portion of bathroom ceiling caved in, where headaches had become much less frequent to point of afflicting her "once in a while," and she was not significantly affected by her injuries in other ways; new trial on damages would be ordered unless parties stipulated to reduce verdict to sum of $25,000. *Vahabe v. Barkus,* 150 A.D.2d 676, 541 N.Y.S.2d 549 (2d Dep't 1989).

Awards of $250,000 in damages to plaintiff and $50,000 in damages to her husband for loss of consortium were not excessive where expert testified that (1) plaintiff suffered from chronic postwhiplash syndrome, vertebral subluxation, and brachia neuralgia, (2) her injuries and pain were permanent and dramatically limited her activities, and (3) she suffered from permanent posttraumatic stress disorder. *Robinson v. Ross,* 180 App. Div. 2d 859, 579 N.Y.S.2d 476 (3d Dep't 1992).

In action for injuries sustained in slip and fall in supermarket, court properly set aside jury award of $15,000 for future pain and suffering, and properly ordered a new trial unless the defendant agreed to the award of $100,000, where (1) plaintiff had been in constant pain since accident, was required to resort to pain relievers, was required to perform isometric exercises daily at two-hour intervals, and wore cervical collar, (2) plaintiff was prevented from doing most activities she used to enjoy, and the limitations affected the plaintiff emotionally, (3) plaintiff's husband testified that she was frequently irritable and tired and that their sex life had suffered, and (4) plaintiff's expert testified that the plaintiff had considerable lack of motion in her back and radiating pain associated with neck motion, and that symptoms would persist even if she had surgery. *Wendell v. Supermarkets Gen. Corp.,* 189 A.D.2d 1063, 592 N.Y.S.2d 895 (3d Dep't 1993).

CHAPTER 7

HEADACHE AND OROFACIAL PAINS, INCLUDING TMJ

§ 7.15 Verdicts and Settlements (New)

The following personal injury cases involve temporomandibular joint (TMJ) injuries:

In a workers' compensation proceeding for neck injuries incurred while performing an extended session of court reporting, the judge's order requiring the defendant to authorize follow-up treatment by a specialist in temporomandibular joint disease would be remanded to permit the testifying orthodontist to clarify his opinion about the relationship, if any, between the work-related injury and claimant's TMJ condition. *Accurate Reporters v. Moore,* 605 So. 2d 585, 17 W.D. Fla. 2278 (Fla. App. 1 1992).

Dentist was entitled to summary judgment dismissing causes of action for products liability and breach of implied warranty which arose when plaintiff was allegedly injured by defective mandibular prosthesis inserted into her mouth during tooth-capping procedure since insertion of such device was merely incidental to medical treatment and did not constitute "sale" of device as required for such causes of action. *Goldfarb v. Teitelbaum,* 149 App. Div. 2d 566, 540 N.Y.S.2d 263 (2d Dep't 1989).

In action in which recipients of temporomandibular joint implants alleged that manufacturer of polytetrafluoroethylene (PTFE), a component of joints, had breached duty to warn them of risks involved in having implants made from PTFE implanted in their jaws, court granted defendant manufacturer's motion for summary judgment where, among other reasons, no statutory or regulatory labeling requirement imposed on manufacturer a duty to warn plaintiffs; PTFE was not "medical device" or "component" of medical device within meaning of Federal Food, Drug, and Cosmetic Act, 21

U.S.C.S. § 321(h), which required manufacturers of medical devices to develop appropriate warnings and to ensure that physicians receive them, when as sold PTFE was not "intended for use in diagnosis of disease or other conditions" or "intended to affect the structure or any function of the body of man." *Anguiano v. E.I. Du Pont de Nemours & Co.,* 808 F. Supp. 719 (D.C. Ariz. 1992).

Motion for summary judgment made by manufacturer of polytetraflouroethylene (PTFE) resins and fibers used in manufacture of Proplast, was denied in negligence and strict liability action based primarily on failure to warn and brought by recipient of temporomandibular joint implant manufactured from Proplast. Plaintiff alleged that implant disintegrated and that she was injured by PTFE particles which remained after disintegration. Plaintiff further contended that PTFE manufacturer was aware of studies questioning propriety of using PTFE to make jaw implants and thus had duty to warn. In its motion for summary judgment, defendant claimed that it played no role in design, manufacture, or sale of implant, that it was merely bulk supplier of raw material and was not aware of buyer's intended use in making implant, and that it had no duty to either ascertain whether buyer's use was safe or to warn of potential dangers. Defendant also argued that since FDA regulated and approved use of PTFE for Proplast implants, it was relieved of any duty and that nevertheless it satisfied any duty it may have had by warning implant manufacturer that PTFE was not made for medical purposes and that it had not conducted any tests. Finally, defendant contended that implant manufacturer had altered PTFE, thus negating strict liability claim. Summary judgment was denied, since as matter of public policy, connection between injury and defendant's actions was not too remote to impose duty to warn, given evidence of defendant's awareness of use and potential risks. Magnitude of risk was substantial so that defendant's reliance on implant manufacturer as intermediary may have been unreasonable. Questions of material fact precluding summary judgment on claims existed concerning defendant's knowledge of medical use and of dangers, whether PTFE was materially altered, and whether disclaimer or warning to implant manufacturer was sufficient. Also, FDA approval was not dispositive, but was only one factor to consider in determining whether defendant had discharged its duty. *Hegna v. E.I. Du Pont de Nemours & Co.,* 806 F. Supp. 822 (D.C. Minn. 1992) (applying Minnesota law).

In consolidation of three products liability actions based on negligence, strict liability, breach of warranty, and misrepresentation, brought against manufacturer of polytetrafluoroethylene (PTFE), trademarked as Teflon, for injuries allegedly sustained as result of use of material in manufacture of plaintiffs' Proplast temporomandibular implants, summary judgment in favor of PTFE manufacturer was granted on all claims. Although claims were also originally brought against manufacturer of implants, no appearance was made by bankrupt company. Plaintiffs alleged that defendant had conclusive knowledge use of PTFE as material used to make Proplast, which in turn was used to make medical devices, had dangerous consequences, and indeed as early as 1967 defendant was aware of studies questioning propriety of so using substance. However, contrary to plaintiffs' assertion, evidence of defendant's apparent knowledge amounted not to conclusive knowledge, but rather concern about lack of knowledge which was expressed to purchasers of substance. Defendant contended that as bulk supplier to medical device manufacturer of FDA-regulated and approved medical device, it had no duty to assume safety of implant designed and manufactured by another. This was enough to relieve defendant, under both negligence and strict liability, of its duty to warn, between which there was no significant difference. Defendant was not supplier of chattels within meaning of § 388 of Restatement of Torts 2d. Moreover, North Dakota Supreme Court would adopt bulk supplier doctrine under which intermediary, not supplier, must provide warnings to ultimate consumers. Doctrine was appropriate since raw materials such as Teflon have many uses, and FDA is ultimately responsible for approval of medical devices and mandates device manufacturer to insure that FDA has all information required for FDA's determination of safety. It was not necessary that jury consider whether PTFE manufacturer acted reasonably in relying on intermediary to provide warnings to ultimate consumer. *Veil v. Vitek, Inc.,* 803 F. Supp. 229 (D.C.N.D. 1992) (applying North Dakota law).

Summary judgment was granted in favor of manufacturer of polytetrafluroethylene (PTFE) fibers in action based on negligence, strict liability, and breach of implied warranty, brought for alleged injuries caused by temporomandibular joint implant containing Proplast. Plaintiff alleged that Proplast was dangerous substance, and affidavit testimony of oral surgeon attributed plaintiff's injuries to use of defendant's teflon component as raw material in making Proplast. Defendant responded that it did not manufacture Proplast, but merely supplied PTFE fibers to Proplast manufacturer which used its own patented procedures to make substance. Also, PTFE fibers had been used for variety of other purposes for many years. Summary judgment was granted since plaintiff failed to provide any evidence that PTFE was negligently manufactured or defective, and also failed to prove that defendant and Proplast manufacturer were joint venturers. (Plaintiff neither alleged nor proved that there was inadequate labeling of PTFE). *Miller v. E.I. Du Pont de Nemours & Co.,* 811 F. Supp. 1286, Prod. Liab. Rep. (CCH) ¶ 13344 (D.C. Tenn. 1992).

Summary judgment was affirmed in favor of manufacturer of polytetrafluoroethylene (PTFE), sold under trademark "Teflon," which is one of principal components of material known as Proplast, which is used in manufacturer of temporomandibular joint (TMJ) implants. Defendant material manufacturer sold Teflon to implant manufacturer, who used Teflon in fabricating Proplast. Proplast was approved by FDA as Class II device for various TMJ-related applications. However, in 1991, FDA ordered recall of material. Under theories of negligence and breach of express and implied warranties, plaintiff alleged that he suffered permanent and irreversible damage to both TMJs as result of bone deterioration in his jaw caused by Proplast; and that PTFE was unfit for use in TMJ implant. Defendant had advised implant manufacturer that PTFE it manufactured was for industrial use; that it had not conducted any studies of use of material for medical purposes; and that those using product for medical purposes must bear full responsibility for results. Court held that suppliers of raw materials that are not inherently defective do not owe duty to assure safety of specialized applications of those materials; and that component manufacturer need not analyze design of completed product which incorporates its nondefective component part. In addition, no express warranties were made by material manufacturer as to suitability of PTFE for medical uses, and implied warranties with respect to such use were effectively disclaimed by defendant's explicit statement that it did not know whether PTFE was reasonably fit for use intended by implant manufacturer. *Nowak v. E.I. Du Pont de Nemours & Co.,* 827 F. Supp. 1334, Prod. Liab. Rep. (CCH) ¶ 13694 (W.D. Mich. 1993) (applying Michigan law).

Judgment for plaintiff, who was awarded $351,385 for injuries sustained in a rear-end collision, was reversed by the Supreme Court of Nebraska, which held that the trial court abused its discretion in denying the defendant's motion to compel a mental examination of the plaintiff by a clinical psychologist. There was evidence that a dentist diagnosed plaintiff's problem, consisting of pain in her jaws and neck, spells of dizziness, diminished hearing, and numbness in her right arm, as a temporomandibular joint dysfunction. An orthopedist that plaintiff's employer required her to see diagnosed an acute cervical sprain. Several physicians who examined the plaintiff found no x-ray or other "objective" physical evidence of the cause for her continuing pain. Although none doubted the existence of the pain, some thought the pain might be the result of a functional overlay—that is, that its etiology was emotional rather than physiological. Based on evidence that there might have been an emotional or psychological component to the plaintiff's pain, the Supreme Court held that her mental condition was in controversy, and the motion to compel a mental examination should have been granted. *Thynne v. Omaha,* 217 Neb. 654, 351 N.W.2d 54 (1984).

Child who was found to be suffering from temporomandibular joint dysfunction shortly after accident was entitled to damages, notwithstanding predisposition to develop condition as result of unfavorable skeletal condition, where evidence established that she had not had any problems or treatment for condition prior to accident, dentist and orthodontist attributed problem to accident, and defendants presented no proof of any other cause for onset of condition. *Breaux v. Maturin,* 619 So. 2d 174 (La. App. 3d 1993).

In personal injury action arising from automobile collision, award of $15,000 for future medical expense was supported by testimony of orthopedist that plaintiff would require at least one year of aggressive physical therapy, three times weekly at cost of approximately $100 per week, to overcome pain and muscle spasms, and by testimony of dentist that surgical realignment of jaw and long-term orthodontic treatment costing between $8,000 and $15,000 was medical probability. *Wyble v. Allstate Ins. Co.,* 581 So. 2d 325 (La. App. 3d 1991).

Award of $10,000 to passenger in automobile that was rear-ended was inadequate; passenger suffered cervical sprain/strain as well as injury that originated in right side of his neck and progressed to his temporomandibular joint. Given inadequate awards for past medical expenses and general damages, total award would be increased to $31,147, which included $5,000 in general damages for cervical sprain/strain and $10,000 in general damages for TMJ dysfunction. *Stoutes v. General Motors Acceptance Corp.*, 598 So. 2d 654 (La. App. 3d 1992).

Zero damage award was error as to woman whose automobile was broadsided by defendant's vehicle, resulting in woman's head impacting and breaking windshield; although evidence of nature and extent of certain injuries to woman's head, neck, and back was conflicting and jury was therefore entitled to infer that these injuries were not compensable, woman presented additional evidence that she developed jaw condition known as temporomandibular joint syndrome (TMJ); this additional evidence included testimony by two oral surgeons who found that woman had sustained injury to her neck muscles that resulted in pain with each movement of her jaw, consistent with condition of TMJ; court erred in failing to instruct jury on loss of future earning capacity. *Martinez v. Shapland,* 833 P.2d 837 (Colo. App. 1992).

CHAPTER 11

PSYCHIATRIC DISORDERS ASSOCIATED WITH CLOSED HEAD INJURY

§ 11.16A —Can Obsessive-Compulsive Disorder Follow Closed Head Injury? (New)

Obsessive-compulsive disorder (OCD) is a disorder characterized by a number of distressing symptoms deriving from recurrent obsessions and/or compulsions. The condition causes severe distress and interferes with all aspects of the individual's life. An *obsession* is a persistent idea, thought, impulse, or image that is experienced as intrusive, inappropriate, and anxiety-provoking. These persons have a preoccupation with becoming contaminated by "germs," and have continuously intrusive thoughts about engaging in behaviors that the person normally views as repugnant (often sexual or aggressive). *Compulsions* are repetitive behaviors such as hand washing, frequent checking, etc., which are "driven" and irresistable; the execution of these behaviors does not provide gratification. Compulsions often derive from obsessional thinking. For example, repetitive thoughts such as killing a person may be followed by intensive and repetitive hand washing, presumably in an attempt to "purge" the mind of such thoughts. OCD can be an extremely disabling condition and it is estimated to occur in approximately 2 percent of the general population. It is probably actually higher than this, since many sufferers are ashamed of being possessed by a condition they view as "crazy," and may not often acknowledge its presence even to health care providers. (Indeed, the idea of possession is interesting; the sufferer often regards his obsessional thinking and repetitive behavior as irrational and somehow ego-alien.)

There may be a biological basis for OCD. Those whose family members have the disorder are 10 times more likely to be afflicted with it. S. Rasmussen et al., "The Epidemiology of Obsessive-Compulsive Disorder," 45 *J. of Clin. Psychiatry,* 450–457 (1984); and S. Turner et al., "Biological Factors in Obsessive-Compulsive Disorder," 97 *Psychology Bulletin,* 430–450 (1958).

Recent imaging studies have strongly implicated a neurologic basis for the disorder. (R. Insel, "Neurobiology of Obsessive-Compulsive Disorder—A Review," 7 *International Clin. Psychopharmacology,* 31–33 (1992). Increased metabolic rates are seen in the left orbital gyrus and in bilateral caudate nuclei, detectible by functional imaging scans which illustrate regional cerebral blood flow (PET). L. Baxter et al., "Local Cerebral Glucose Metabolic Rates in Obsessive-Compulsive Disorder," 44 *Archives of Gen. Psychiatry,* 211–219 (1987). These studies provide evidence for a neurological basis for OCD. Reports of this disorder emerging from brain tumors have appeared in the medical literature. J. Seibyl et al., "Obsessive-Compulsive Symptoms in a Patient with a Right Frontal Lobe Lesion," 1 *Neuropsychiatry, Neuropsychology & Behavioral Neurology,* 295–299 (1989), S. Swedo et al., "High Prevalence of Obsessive-Compulsive Symptoms in Patients with Sydenham's Chorea," 146 *Am. J. Psychiatry,* 246–249 (1989). In earlier editions of this text, the phenomenon of OCD following head trauma was not discussed. Nevertheless, I have seen, over many years, four cases where OCD quite clearly followed relatively mild head trauma (involving only transient loss of consciousness and a brief period of posttraumatic amnesia). In none of these cases was there a family history of OCD or any suggestion that the individual's personality was predisposed to the development of such a disorder. The head injury literature is beginning to report the development of obsessive-compulsive disorder following head injury. J. McKeon et al., "Obsessive-Compulsive Neurosis Following Head Injury—A Report of Four Cases," 144 *Brit. J. Psychiatry,* 190–192 (1984); W. Lashman, "Brain Damage in Relation to Psychiatric Disability After Head Injury," 114 *Brit. J. Psychiatry,* 373–410 (1968); R. Kant et al., "Obsessive-Compulsive Disorder After Closed Head Injury: Review of Literature and Report of Four Cases," 10(1) *Brain Injury,* 55–63 (1996). The cases discussed in the literature, and in those encountered in my practice, had no prior history of a significant psychiatric disorder.

How can this happen? It is at least theoretically possible that the development of these symptoms may occur in individuals who, while having no prior history of psychiatric disorder, are preoccupied with the affective and cognitive symptoms that follow injury. Many persons who have had a significant head injury become depressed. In all four of the patients I have seen, and in those described by Kant and colleagues, the individuals were depressed.

Considering an organic etiology, based in brain tissue impairment, as being responsible for the development of OCD, we should remember that most closed head injuries result in diffuse, rather than focal, injury. Head injury very often affects the orbital frontal cortex, probably as a result of the brain contusing itself against the corrugations on the underlying skull. Behavioral disorders based on frontal lobe pathology, as we have noted frequently, including aggression, impulsive sexuality, and a variety of other syndromes, are well described and are dealt with in **Chapter 3.** Nevertheless, the development of OCD following head injury cannot be a particularly common event, although this may be due at least in part to under-reporting since, as we have mentioned, such individuals are ashamed of their disorder and may not describe it to caregivers or even to relatives. Clinical psychiatrists are aware of this characteristic of patients with OCD, and it is often surprising how well such individuals succeed in hiding their disorder from significant others.

I cannot prove it, but my sense is that the development of OCD following head injury derives from parenchymal damage rather than being psychogenic.

Since this condition is now beginning to be reported by clinicians, we will carefully watch its elucidation in the developing literature.

§ 11.28 Verdicts and Settlements (New)

The following personal injury cases involve personality change as a result of closed head trauma:

In *Lee's Mobile Wash v. Campbell,* 853 P.2d 1140 (Colo. 1993), the plaintiff was involved in a rear end car accident in which he testified that his head hit both the rear window of his truck cab and the steering wheel. After considerable physical and mental testing to determine the nature and extent of his injuries, he presented the testimony of three psychologists, including one neuropsychologist, that he had suffered mild to moderate cerebral dysfunction caused by the accident, was experiencing significant memory deficit, anger, and mild depression, and was not malingering. This testimony was further bolstered by several lay witnesses, including the plaintiff and his wife, who testified that the plaintiff exhibited negative changes in both memory and personality after the accident. In contrast, the defendant's expert witness, who was a psychiatrist, testified that plaintiff had some minor to mild brain impairment from the car accident, which he defined as having experienced a period of unconsciousness or posttraumatic amnesia lasting between 30 minutes and 24 hours. Although finding that the defendant was responsible for some injury to the plaintiff, the jury determined that, under the state's rules for recovery of damages beyond the no-fault insurance thresholds, the jury awarded no "noneconomic" damages. In upholding the decision, the court emphasized that its duty was to reconcile the verdict with the evidence if that was at all possible. Here, the reconciliation was very possible since the jury reasonably could have concluded that the plaintiff's impairment due to the accident lasted only minutes and was de minimis.

In *McDonald v. Lincoln U-Cart Concrete Co.,* 232 Neb. 960, 442 N.W.2d 892 (1989), the victim was 18 years old when he was injured in a collision between his motorcycle and an automobile. He suffered a severe head injury, which caused a complete change in his personality. The victim's postaccident behavior included a tendency to make improper remarks and funny faces, and to not make sense "sometimes." He also tired easily, was not as alert as he once was, talked to himself, and was emotionally unstable. The victim's father tried to bring him back into one of the family businesses, but he worked only briefly at his father's liquor store before leaving, because he did not get along with fellow employees, got into "problems with customers," was "confused on selling," and generally did not perform well. The father placed him in business dealing with signs and concrete, but the victim could not cope with the tasks incident to those jobs and left them both. He began working with the rehabilitation services division of the state's department of education, but during the training program, the victim displayed regression and lack of emotional tolerance when he was switched from one job to another, swore under his breath, made other comments, exhibited inappropriate behavior when working with the public, and made faces. The victim ended up unemployed for a prolonged period after finishing the rehabilitation program, and at the time of the proceeding to be declared totally disabled for workers' compensation purposes, worked only 16 to 18 hours per week at a restaurant clearing tables and bathrooms, and scraping gum from the undersides of tables.

In *Slaughter v. Slaughter,* 499 So. 2d 1123 (La. App. 3d 1986), a divorce case in which the brain injury victim's altered personality apparently contributed to the disintegration of his marriage, and resulted in a judicial finding that the victim's changed personality traits, along with several other factors, warranted restriction of his child visitation rights.

In *Lynch v. Board of Educ.,* 82 Ill. 2d 415, 45 Ill. Dec. 96, 412 N.E.2d 447 (1980), a case in which psychiatric treatment and medication were recommended to help control the behavior of the plaintiff, whose brain damage was believed permanent and irreversible; plaintiff's personality after being injured in a "powder puff" football game was described as having changed to one of irritability, rebelliousness, and moodiness.

In *Twait v. Olson,* 104 Ill. App. 3d 191, 60 Ill. Dec. 345, 432 N.E.2d 1244 (3d Dist. 1982), a $500,000 award to 17-year-old male injured in automobile accident, with irreparable brain injury resulting in lowered intelligence and altered personality, where plaintiff, who had 50.5-year life expectancy, suffered impaired space perception, speech, and coordination, and was totally unable to be employed or to care for himself.

In *Jackson v. United States,* 526 F. Supp. 1149 (E.D. Ark. 1981), an award of $275,000 to 60-year-old man with life expectancy of only 15 years, who during surgery suffered permanent brain damage affecting all areas of emotional and physical behavior; the plaintiff required full-time care and was transformed from a personable, intelligent, and active person to the status of invalid with subnormal intelligence and severe personality disorder.

In *Stanley v. Wiley,* 325 So. 2d 661 (La. App. 3d 1975), a $275,000 award to 13-year-old girl who sustained brain damage in automobile accident, along with broken pelvis; in addition to emotional management problems, permanent brain damage resulted in mental retardation or intellectual impairment to dull-normal range, impairment of judgment and memory; loss and repression of memory, psychosomatic scalp pains, bedwetting, fear of being alone and of riding in automobiles, and some physical impairment of skilled movement.

CHAPTER 12

NEUROPSYCHOLOGY IN BRAIN INJURY INVESTIGATION

§ 12.23 Verdicts and Settlements

The following head trauma cases involve mental or neurological conditions:

In *Scarberry v. Ohio River Co.,* 217 F. Supp. 189 (D.C. W. Va. 1963), a towboat oiler's suit under the Jones Act for personal injuries sustained when a guard railing gave way as the oiler was ascending to the main deck of the towboat, causing the oiler to fall backward and strike his head severely against the port engine, the court found that there was no organic brain damage or permanent injury as a result of the accident, but that the accident aggravated the oiler's pre-existing anxiety complex. The court said that the oiler had had headaches in prior years, was punished for bad conduct while in the Navy, had had trouble with prior employers, and did not score high in intelligence tests, but that for six years before the accident he had been a steady and satisfactory employee. After the accident, the oiler had a definite loss of memory, headaches, fatigue, a poor tolerance for exertion, and an anxiety reaction that made him depressed. Rejecting the defendant's contention that the oiler's disability was due in whole or in part to worry about the loss or abolition of his job, his financial condition, or his son's educational problems, the court ordered judgment entered for the oiler in the amount of $11,600.

The evidence in *Lee v. Stevens,* 251 N.C. 429, 111 S.E.2d 623 (1959), was held insufficient to support the jury's finding that a woman's cerebral hemorrhage five weeks after an automobile accident was the result of the accident rather than pre-existing conditions. She testified that her pre-accident physical condition was "perfect"; that she continued working after the accident, but her head hurt her all the time, with headaches starting on the back of her head and moving to the top of her head; and that after the accident she also suffered from nausea, vomiting, and nervousness. About five weeks after the accident she suffered a cerebral hemorrhage or stroke. Her doctor testified that there was a "possibility" that a blow received in the accident caused the hemorrhage, but he found no evidence of skull fracture, and stated that a cerebral hemorrhage is "extremely infrequent" in the absence of a skull fracture. He also testified that the woman had been hospitalized for high blood pressure or hypertension before the accident; that absent a skull fracture, trauma is the least of all causes of cerebral hemorrhage; that disease of the blood vessels accounts for the greatest proportion of cerebral hemorrhages; and that the woman's hemorrhage "had been building up for some time." A neurological surgeon, testifying for the defendants, stated that the most common causes of cerebral hemorrhage are rupture of a congenital aneurysm of the brain, or a weak wall in a blood vessel, and high blood pressure, or defective areas in blood vessel walls associated therewith; that nausea, dizziness, and headaches are symptoms of a variety of other illnesses associated with the brain; and that his opinion was that the woman had a cerebral hemorrhage due either to a ruptured aneurysm or to high blood pressure. In setting aside a judgment based on a $16,000 jury verdict in the woman's favor, the court said that "the evidence was insufficient to show causal relationship between the plaintiff's injury in the accident and the cerebral hemorrhage five weeks later."

The jury in *Kwiatkowski v. John Lowry, Inc.*, 248 App. Div. 459, 290 N.Y.S. 627 (1936), was held not justified in finding that a carpenter foreman's pre-existing brain tumor was "lit-up" by a hemorrhage following a head blow, resulting in his death. The foreman had a brain tumor before the incident and had been treated for headaches. He struck his head on a projecting 2 by 4 as he stooped to pass under a canvas, throwing him to his knees. He remained at work that day and continued working for several days thereafter, but died 27 days after the incident. The physician who performed the autopsy found a localized growth about the size of a walnut encapsulated in the left temporal lobe. He testified that it showed evidence of hemorrhage of recent origin, and, together with other experts called by plaintiff, testified that a person may have a benign tumor for many years without suffering inconvenience, and that the "lighting up" of the tumor by the blow was a competent producing cause of death. A doctor who examined the foreman 21 days after the incident found no external evidence of injury, and a neurological examination disclosed no abnormal findings. A doctor who examined part of the tumor removed during the autopsy found no ruptured blood vessels and no hemorrhage, but merely a condition common in any form of brain tumor, and testified, together with another doctor, that if there had been a rupture of the blood vessels unconsciousness would result, and that the blow did not contribute to the foreman's death. In reversing a judgment based on a jury verdict in favor of the foreman's executrix, the court said that the jury's finding that the blow was the cause of his death was against the weight of the evidence.

In *Smith v. Kenosha Auto Transport,* 226 F. Supp. 771 (D.C. Mont. 1964) (applying Montana law), the trial court denied the defendants' alternative motions for judgment notwithstanding the verdict or for a new trial in a suit arising out of a head-on collision between an empty automobile transport and a truck, in which both vehicles were demolished and the truck driver suffered a fractured right arm, bruises and cuts on his arms and legs, and cuts and injuries on his face and head. The driver, who was then 34 years old, was rendered unconscious and vaguely remembered being brought to a hospital, where he again lapsed into unconsciousness. After several months he attempted to return to work, but was forced to quit because of pain and discomfort and "spells" which he found difficult to describe, but which doctors diagnosed as epileptic seizure of the petit mal type. In addition to being unable to work, the driver's personality changed so that he withdrew from all social contacts, his oldest daughter left home because of his treatment of her, and his wife became afraid to leave the younger children alone in his care. He sat throughout the several days of the trial staring and unmoving and almost rigid. While his speech was rational and coherent when he testified, he was hesitant and slow to answer, and seemingly had difficulty in comprehending the questions and formulating the answers. The medical evidence, which was largely uncontradicted, was that after the accident the driver suffered both from physical brain damage demonstrable by pneumoencephalogram and manifesting itself in petit mal epileptic seizures, and from a psychological disorder. There was evidence that before the accident the driver was happy and enthusiastic about his work, happy and congenial in his relationships with his family and friends, and was considered to be a better than average truck driver and a willing and able worker. About a year before the accident, however, the driver suffered a nervous disorder, said to result from association with his brother, and he consulted a neurosurgeon, who prescribed medication and rest. The doctor diagnosed the condition as a possible paroxysmal disorder, but the driver responded to the treatment, was released by the doctor, and returned to work in about six weeks. From this evidence, the court said, the jury could find that the driver's postaccident condition was caused by the accident and did not predate the accident, despite the previous diagnosis of a convulsive disorder.

A trial court's findings that a blow to a longshoreman's head did not aggravate his pre-existing grand mal epilepsy, but temporarily aggravated his pre-existing personality disorder, was upheld in *Smith v. Jugoslavenska Linijska Plovidea,* 278 F.2d 176 (4th Cir. Va. 1960), in which a ship's ladder swung away from the hatch coaming as the longshoreman was descending it, drawing him to the 'tween deck below where he struck his head and was knocked unconscious. When he regained consciousness in a hospital, he was in a raging and maniacal condition. There was evidence that the longshoreman had suffered convulsive seizures, with some degree of regularity, since the age of 6, and that he had had no convulsive seizures for about 2 years before the accident, but about 12 days after the accident had a seizure while in the hospital. Army records showed that the longshoreman received a medical discharge from the Army in 1946 for "epilepsy, grand mal, psychomotor," and was given a 100 percent disability pension, later reduced to 50 percent of the original amount; that he was drafted again in 1952; that in 1953 he was given electroencephalogram (EEG) tests, which indicated a "border slow" record, and on the basis of these tests the 1946 diagnosis of epilepsy grand mal was held untenable, the new diagnosis being "hysteroid phenomena under frustration" and "'temper tantrum' rather than psychomotor epilepsy"; and that in 1956 it was decided that the 1953 diagnosis, then spoken of as "passive-aggressive personality, aggressive type," was unmistakably erroneous, and the sole diagnosis was epilepsy grand mal and severe psychomotor attacks. The respondent vessel's two experts testified that since the convulsive seizures were about as frequent before as after the accident, they could not say that the accident aggravated the epilepsy. One of them testified, however, that the longshoreman's personality disorder would have been aggravated by the accident. In upholding a $5,750 decree in the longshoreman's favor, the court said that the diagnosis of a temporarily aggravated personality disorder adequately explained the longshoreman's condition and behavior after the accident.

A jury was held justified in finding a causal connection between a blow on the head and subsequent mental illness in *Evans v. S.J. Groves & Sons Co.,* 315 F.2d 335 (2d Cir. 1963), where a truck in which a 57-year-old woman was riding was struck by an approaching truck which skidded into the wrong lane, lifting the woman out of her seat and causing her head to strike the windshield, resulting in a bump on the top of her head one-half to three-quarters of an inch high and two-and-one-half to three inches long. Four days later she consulted her local physician, complaining of tiredness, dizziness, fainting spells, and "blinking spells of vision," but neither she nor her doctor attached much significance to the accident because she had previously complained of dizziness, grogginess, and false and defective hearing. Two weeks later she again saw her doctor, complaining of head symptoms, and from that time forward her condition progressively worsened, ending with her commitment, as a legally adjudged incompetent, in a state hospital for the mentally ill. There was evidence that at the time of the accident the woman suffered from a diseased middle ear, which caused her hearing difficulties, but the defendant's prime theory was that she suffered from a brain tumor which produced the head symptoms evidenced before the impact. The plaintiff's case was that the collision caused thrombosis of the left lateral sinus, resulting in intracranial pressure. There was medical evidence that thrombosis, or blockage, of the sinus can be caused either by ear disease or by head injury; that both causes are common ones; and that the condition can develop when circulation is at a low ebb from any cause. In affirming a judgment in the plaintiff's favor, the court said that the jury could infer that both the head injury and the ear disease cooperated to bring about intracranial pressure, even though no medical expert testified specifically as to the possibility of such cooperative causation, since "it must be expected that juries will occasionally provide news for doctors."

The jury in *Ross v. Duluth, Missabe & Iron Range R. Co.,* 207 Minn. 157, 290 N.W. 566 (1940), was held justified in finding that a railroad worker's insanity, for which he was committed about two months after a railroad accident, was caused by the accident rather than by preexisting conditions. There was evidence that the worker was thrown to the ground in a railroad collision, rendering him unconscious; that when he regained consciousness he was dizzy and felt a pounding sensation in his head; that a lump appeared on his temple, gradually changing to a scar; that about six weeks after the accident he was afflicted with fainting spells and gastric hemorrhages; and that shortly thereafter he was committed because of insanity. It was undisputed that before the accident he appeared to be normal in all respects, but that shortly after the accident he became profane in his language and irritable of disposition, his hands trembled so that he had difficulty eating, he became untidy in appearance, he purchased articles which he could not afford and did not need, and in other ways he evidenced a lack of judgment. The railroad's medical witnesses ascribed the worker's condition to physical defects incident to old age, particularly arteriosclerosis, a failing heart, and accompanying high blood pressure. The plaintiff's medical witnesses conceded that insanity could be caused by these conditions, but they questioned the findings of a failing heart and unduly high blood pressure, gave their opinion that the worker's insanity was not caused by such conditions, and advanced the theory that his mental condition was due to the replacement of brain cells by scarred tissue resulting because of tiny hemorrhages in the frontal lobe of the brain, caused by the head injury sustained in the collision. In affirming a $15,000 judgment in the worker's favor, the court said that considered as a whole, the medical testimony raised a question of fact for the jury.

The jury in *Montgomery Ward & Co. v. Callahan,* 127 F.2d 32 (10th Cir. 1942), was held to have properly found that a woman's insanity resulted from a blow received in a store when she was struck by a 250-pound roll of linoleum, as against the store's contention that she suffered from hereditary dementia praecox not resulting from the blow. The woman alleged that she was struck and crushed to the floor by the roll of linoleum, suffering, among other injuries, a brain concussion and bruises about the head, face, chest, shoulders, back, and spine; that prior to the accident she was in good health; and that as a result of the accident she would continue to suffer constant pain and anguish, and was rendered hopelessly and permanently insane. She offered the testimony of a specialist in mental and nervous diseases that a blow can be the sole cause of any mental deterioration, including dementia praecox or other form of insanity. In answer to a hypothetical question, she further stated that the blow would be the cause of her condition. In an effort to show the hereditary nature of the woman's disease, the store introduced testimony showing that the woman had a number of near relatives who were insane, and offered the testimony of a number of medical experts that the woman was suffering from dementia praecox and that dementia praecox is functional and will not result from trauma. In affirming a judgment based on a jury verdict in the woman's favor, the court said that the jury chose to believe the woman's testimony and that the verdict was not without the support of competent testimony.

The question whether the recurrence of a 51-year-old bachelor's mental disorder after an automobile accident was caused by the accident or was purely coincidental was an important issue in *Levy v. Indemnity Ins. Co.,* 8 So. 2d 774 (La. App. 1942), where 25, 17, 13, and 10 years before the accident in suit he suffered from mental disorders then diagnosed as dementia praecox. He was treated after each incident and was discharged, not as permanently well, but as being in such mental condition as to warrant release. During the 10-year interval before the accident, he resumed normal living and habits, procured gainful employment, was economical and saved money, and according to his closest associates was entirely normal, although a member of a sanitarium staff testified that he was regarded as being "queer" during that period, reflecting the characteristics peculiar to one who has gone through episodes of insanity. In the accident, the car in which the bachelor was riding left the road and overturned, knocking the bachelor unconscious for 12 hours with a blow to the back of his head, causing many contusions, lacerating his scalp, and injuring the spinous process of the seventh cervical vertebra. Within a few days, he began to act queerly and was admitted to a veterans' hospital with a mental disorder diagnosed as manic-depressive psychosis. There was evidence that it is exceedingly difficult to distinguish between dementia praecox and manic-depressive psychosis; that scientists have not determined the exact original cause of either affliction; that the most common causes for recurrence are psychic trauma, grief, sorrow, and brooding; that recurrence will take place without known reasons; and that recurrence is more frequent and of greater duration as the patient advances in years. The physicians who testified were divided as to whether physical trauma will bring about a recurrence of either condition, but it was established that a patient's anxiety and brooding over his condition, and a fear of a return to insanity, can cause a recurrence. One doctor testified that the main cause of the bachelor's recurrence was his fear that he might not be restored to sanity. Another doctor was of the opinion that the injury was the exciting and precipitating cause of the recurrence. The court concluded that there was a direct causal connection between the accident and the recurrence of the bachelor's mental disorder.

Trial court properly refused to give instruction on aggravation of plaintiff's preexisting latent neurological brain disorder which allegedly resulted in organic schizophrenia, where testimony showed plaintiff had not suffered head trauma in auto accident. *Klanseck v. Anderson Sales & Service, Inc.,* 136 Mich. App. 75, 356 N.W.2d 275 (1984).

The jury in *Faulhaber v. Griswold,* 124 Neb. 357, 246 N.W. 727 (1933), was held warranted in finding that a girl's insanity resulted from a collision between a truck and an automobile in which she was a passenger, rather than to have preexisted. There was evidence that in the collision the girl was thrown forward and received a bump on the top of her head; that almost immediately thereafter she suffered from shock, fright, and severe headaches; that thereafter she became extremely nervous; that within a few days she manifested mental disturbance; and that within a few weeks thereafter she was committed to a state hospital for the insane, where she remained at the time of trial. The defendant's evidence was that the girl suffered from dementia praecox; that dementia praecox is an inherited mental disease; and that the injury, shock, and fright resulting from the accident did not cause or contribute to her condition. The girl's medical experts testified that she might have gone through life without ever developing dementia praecox but for the injury, and that the injury, shock, and fright caused the development of the disease. In affirming a judgment in the girl's favor, the court said that the question whether her mental condition resulted from the accident was a question of fact for the jury.

The question whether a railroad passenger's condition resulted from traumatic neurasthenia sustained in a railroad accident, or from preexisting rheumatism and Bright's disease, was the principal issue in *Lee v. Kansas City Southern R. Co.,* 220 F. 863 (8th Cir. 1915), where the train on which the passenger was riding ran through an open switch and collided with some cars on a sidetrack. The passenger testified that in the collision his head struck some object and his neck was wrenched so that he felt something "slip or pop and give way," producing severe pain where the neck joins the head; that he felt dazed and as though a heavy weight were attached to his feet; that his pains continued after the accident; and that about two years later his head became drawn to one side, and he was unable to support it with his neck muscles, and his right arm became partially paralyzed; but that beginning about 3½ years after the accident his health began to improve. The passenger's doctor testified that he treated the passenger for rheumatism before the accident; that by the time of the accident the passenger had recovered from a previous rheumatic attack; and that in his opinion the passenger suffered from traumatic neurasthenia caused by the accident. A great body of contrary evidence, consisting of testimony of the passenger's admissions that he was not injured by the accident, his actions after the accident, and the testimony of physicians who repeatedly examined him, and of other witnesses, to the effect that he was not injured by the collision, and that whatever he suffered was the result of Bright's disease and of rheumatism, was offered, but the court said that a review of the entire evidence showed that a jury question was presented as to whether or not the passenger's sufferings were caused by the collision, and that the trial court erred in instructing a verdict against the passenger.

A sufficient causal connection between a blow to a woman's head and her mental illness to justify a jury verdict in her favor was found in *Allen v. Indemnity Ins. Co.,* 137 So. 2d 110 (La. App. 1962), where the woman sat in a theater seat without a back, fell backward and struck her head, hurting her neck and causing nausea. After the accident a general practitioner found that she was suffering from a cervical strain and a sacroiliac strain, but an orthopedic specialist and a neurological surgeon who subsequently examined her found nothing physically wrong with her. About 8 months after the accident she was examined by a psychiatrist, who found that she was emotionally disturbed, and on the next day she was admitted to a hospital where she received 11 electroshock treatments. She was discharged about 2 weeks after entering the hospital, but received more of these treatments as an outpatient for about 3 more weeks. Four months later she reentered a hospital and received a milder form of treatment consisting of medication and subshock insulin treatment. The woman's psychiatrist testified that in his opinion she developed a nervous condition as a natural consequence of the injuries sustained from her brain concussion in the theater. Two other psychiatrists examined her at the defendant's request. One testified that she suffered from psychasthenic depression originating in her early childhood, which probably had more to do with her trouble than the accident, and that the accident could only be a "precipitating factor" of her condition. The other psychiatrist testified that the woman had an unstable personality with strong obsessive compulsive traits and that in his opinion neither her psychiatric status at the time of trial nor the depressive episode for which she was treated were related to the head injury, since her type of illness is commonly found in patients in the absence of trauma. He concluded that the head injury was more incidentally than causally related to her condition. According to the woman's friends, she was a jolly and energetic person before the accident but thereafter was nervous and had crying spells. After considering the medical and lay testimony, the court concluded that there was sufficient evidence to support the jury's finding that the accident was a "precipitating factor" in the woman's mental illness.

A jury question was held presented in *Walters v. Smith,* 222 Md. 62, 158 A.2d 619 (1960), as to whether a married woman's neurological injuries were sustained in an automobile accident. Before the accident the woman suffered head injuries which occasioned headaches, dizziness, and speech difficultics, diagnosed six years before the accident as caused by a carotid artery smaller than normal, which markedly impaired the blood supply to the brain. An operation was then performed to dilate the arteries on the left side of her brain and to establish circulation, but the result was a complete occlusion of the carotid artery, with partial paralysis of the right side and aphasia. She gradually improved over the years, and at the time of the accident her speech was almost normal, and she no longer needed a brace for her leg, had good movement and strength in her right arm, was able to flex her right foot, exhibited good memory patterns, had no complaints of skull or back pain, and was cheerful and mentally alert. In the automobile collision she was thrown forward against the front seat, hurting her right foot and ankle and her right shoulder, and snapping her neck. There were no fractures, and the foot injury was diagnosed as a sprain. Thereafter she began to have severe headaches and dizzy spells, lost her ability to talk, was nervous, and could not add, substract, or do her housework. One month after the accident she was hospitalized and stellate ganglion blocks were done to increase the sympathetic blood supply to the brain. Her speech improved, as did her neck pain, but months later her right arm and leg were still considerably affected and her headaches continued. The doctor who performed this operation testified that the snapping of her neck impaired her already weakened circulatory system and brought about the speech disturbance and the functional disturbance of the left side of her brain which affected her right arm and leg and aggravated the preexisting condition. On cross-examination, he testified that the woman's background made it reasonable to foresee that over the years her symptoms would become worse or repeat themselves. Concluding that the trial judge erred in directing a verdict for the defendants, the court said that the woman showed at least a reasonable probability that the defendants' negligence caused the condition she was in after the accident.

In *McClintock v. Allen,* 30 Wash. 2d 272, 191 P.2d 679 (1948), arising out of an intersectional automobile collision, a jury was held warranted in finding that the driver of one of the cars suffered brain damage resulting from the accident rather than as a result of the driver's nervous condition before the accident. There was evidence that at the time of the accident the driver was 22 years old, married, weighed 183 pounds, and was strong and healthy, although of a nervous temperament. The driver testified that in the accident he struck his head against the metal frame of the right-hand door; that he was not rendered unconscious, but "everything went flooey" and he did not get out of the car until about five minutes after the impact; that after the accident, he frequently suffered from headaches, nausea, and nosebleeds, and at times had spells of vomiting and spitting up phlegm; that these conditions constantly worsened; and that he had dizzy spells and insomnia, and suffered from continual jerking in his sleep, and gradually lost weight until he had lost 44 pounds by the time of trial. The driver's doctor, a specialist in neurology and brain surgery, testified that he originally diagnosed the case as one of traumatic neurosis, and that when the driver did not improve after treatments for traumatic neurosis, he changed his diagnosis and concluded that it presented a case for brain surgery, owing to a clot in the brain or an accumulation of blood or fluid between the coverings of that organ, caused by the injury. Another physician corroborated this diagnosis. The defendant introduced evidence that at the time and place of the accident, and at another time and place, the driver had a nervous attack or fit; that on each occasion he declared that the attack was due to his previous war service; and that the driver admitted to the defendant's medical witness that he "had had bad nervous symptoms for some time before his discharge" from the Coast Guard. The driver denied making these statements. In affirming a $10,000 judgment in the driver's favor, the court said that the evidence presented a controverted question of fact for the jury and not for the court to decide.

The evidence in *Wooley v. Great Atlantic & Pacific Tea Co.,* 281 F.2d 78 (3d Cir. 1960), was held to justify the jury's finding that a 4-year-old boy's crossed eyes, and his emotional and personality difficulties, were not the proximate result of a glancing blow to the boy's head when a 10-ounce can of tomato soup, which had been stacked with other soup cans in a pyramid fashion in the defendant's supermarket, fell on the boy's head. The plaintiff contended that as a result of the accident the boy's eyes crossed and he suffered emotional difficulties and personality changes. An ophthalmologist testified that before the accident the boy had a "fusional weakness" and that the accident was the precipitating cause of the esotropia, or crossed eyes. A psychiatrist testified that "some minor behavior abnormalities existed prior to the accident"; that the accident "was in a manner of speaking the instrument that broke the camel's back"; and that the accident "was not a causative thing, but it did enhance and set up a cycle." In affirming a judgment based on a verdict awarding $1,700 to the boy and $300 to his mother, over their contention that the damages were inadequate, the court said that the causation issue was for the jury, "in view of the testimony of plaintiff's own medical experts that other factors could have caused the minor plaintiff's physical and psychiatric conditions."

In action alleging that sole cause of plaintiff's narcolepsy was blow to the head she suffered when telephone booth door was opened suddenly, where plaintiff's expert specifically testified that other accidents did not cause or contribute to her condition and defendants' expert testified unequivocally that narcolepsy could not be caused by any blow to the head, whether jury accepted plaintiff's theory or that of defendants they could not have found that other accidents contributed to causation of plaintiff's narcolepsy. *Falkenthal v. Public Bldg. Comm.,* 111 Ill. App. 3d 703, 67 Ill. Dec. 262, 444 N.E.2d 498 (1982) .

The evidence in *Phoenix Amusement Co. v. Padgett's Administratrix,* 301 Ky. 338, 192 S.W.2d 105 (1946), was held insufficient to present a jury question as to whether a girl's brain abscess resulted from a head blow in a fall on theater stairs or an earlier assault upon her. About two weeks before the theater accident the girl suffered a severe injury to her head and eye in an assault upon her by a stranger. Her companion at the time of the theater accident testified that as she was descending the theater stairs she tripped and struck her head on the railing. A physician who performed an autopsy after the girl's death testified that the abscess which caused death was the result of a traumatic injury, and that the abscess could have happened one month, or five or six months, before the girl's death. In reversing a judgment based on a jury verdict in favor of the girl's administratrix, the court said that the evidence raised no more than a speculation that the abscess was the result of the theater accident.

Plaintiff who was struck on head by pipe failed to show that impotence and headaches he suffered were caused by accident, where expert evidence revealed that plaintiff was alcoholic which could have caused his sexual problem, and that he had suffered migraine headaches prior to accident. *Doucet v. B & R Petroleum Services, Inc.,* 546 So. 2d 626 (La. App. 3d 1989).

The jury in *Brannan v. Shertzer,* 242 Minn. 277, 64 N.W.2d 755 (1954), was held warranted in finding that a 58-year-old seamstress' nervous disorders preexisted and did not result from an automobile accident wherein the car in which she was a passenger was struck from behind, causing her to strike her head on the car's window post. She was taken to a hospital where the record showed no unconsciousness but some "lightheadedness" and a "two centimeter hematoma in the right occipital region." Her skin was intact, and a neurological examination was negative. She was examined by a neurologist about 11 weeks after the accident, with essentially negative findings. A psychologist who then examined her testified that she had some impairment of memory and also impairment in the field of abstract perception, and that his findings were consistent with a diagnosis of organic brain damage. Thereafter, she was reexamined by the neurologist, who diagnosed her trouble as posttrauma syndrome, with considerable depression affecting her personality very markedly. He also expressed the opinion that she had suffered a brain concussion with damage to the brain cells. However, she told both the neurologist and the psychologist that after the accident she had headaches, was nervous, was unable to perform her work, lacked confidence in herself, was dizzy, depressed, and tired, and suffered from loss of memory, and that before the accident she had none of these symptoms. The defendant introduced evidence that before the accident she was nervous, had a speech impediment, was subject to crying spells, and at times was irritable or depressed. In affirming a judgment based on a jury verdict awarding her only $793 for her personal injuries and for damage to her car, the court said that the jury could find that except for minor injuries, "her symptoms and ailments antedated the accident and were in no way related to it."

CHAPTER 13

SEQUELAE OF HEAD INJURIES: OUTCOME STUDIES

§ 13.8A —What Accounts for Delayed Recovery from Mild Head Injury? (New)

This is one of the more difficult questions to answer, since so many complex variables are involved in recovery from any injury, not just head injury. In fact, some of the more chronic disorders known to clinicians include fibromyalgia, myofascial pain, posttraumatic headache, back pain, and other conditions associated with "whiplash" and with all kinds of musculoskeletal injuries.

Similarly, both the cognitive and emotional symptoms, as well as the other affective or "vegetative" symptoms that are sequelae of head injury, such as fatigability, insomnia, headaches, dizziness, personality, cognitive, and affective change, etc., often assume a chronic course following head injury.

Sections 13.7 and **13.8** deal with those emotional conditions which predispose to chronicity in many forms of physical disease. Certainly, depression and anxiety, even in very severe forms, are under-diagnosed in the general population. Thus, a previous diagnosis of these conditions is not necessarily indicative of their presence in a particular individual. In fact, most individuals do not receive psychotherapy or pharmacotherapy for these conditions, in spite of their prevalence.

While we have discussed, in §§ **4.3** and **4.23,** the role of psychogenicity in perpetuating symptoms, there remain a significant number of cases in whom prior evidence of psychopathology is difficult to elicit. In many of these cases, one is obliged to conclude that physical processes have been set into motion as a result of the head injury which have caused permanent alterations in brain functioning. An interesting model for the persistence of symptoms following mild and moderate head injury is that of Hayes and colleagues. These investigators describe an "excitotoxic hypothesis." R. Hayes et al., Neurochemical Mechanisms of Mild and Moderate Head Injury: Implications for Treatment in Mild Head Injury 54–79 (H. Levin et al., eds. Oxford University Press, New York 1989). They suggest that, following head injury, there is an excessive release of the neurotransmitter acetylcholine as well as other "excitatory" neurotransmitters. Acetylcholine thus liberated binds to cholinergic receptors on nerve cells, which in turn results in both transient and long-term, even irreversible, changes in the function of that nerve cell. Diffuse axonal injury (DIA) is the principal mechanism of shear injury to the brain. Many axons are clearly damaged by the process of acceleration-deceleration, as revealed by the work of Povlishock and others. J. Povlishock, "The Morphopathologic Responses to Experimental Head Injuries of Varying Severity," in D. Becker & J. Povlishock, eds., "Central Nervous System Status Report 1985," 443–452, sponsored by NINCDS (Byrd Press, Richmond, Va. 1985); J. Povlishock, "Traumatically Induced Axonal Damage Without Concomitant Change in Focally Related Neuronal Stomata and Dendrites," 70 *Acta Neuropathology* 53–59 (1986). If the excitotoxic hypothesis is correct, then maladaptive changes in cellular functioning (while permitting the cell to perform metabolic activity) could explain the persistence of abnormal cognitive processing. If increased levels of acetylcholine are injurious to brain cells, and if free choline persists in the brain tissue following injury, one might expect that anti-cholinergic medications would be beneficial in central nervous system injury. Such treatments have not been consistently reported as efficacious and, in fact, many drugs possessing anti-cholinergic activity (such as tricyclic antidepressants) can actually worsen cognitive performance.

Furthermore, supporters of the so-called "excitotoxic" theory, as far as I can determine, provide no explanation as to why only *some* individuals, even with quite severe injuries, persist in having profound cognitive and emotional changes while others appear to recover completely. Perhaps variations in genetic susceptibility of brain cells to free acetylcholine explain this phenomenon, but that must remain a theoretical consideration until more definitive research proves otherwise. In the meantime, however, my review of the literature leads me to conclude the following: (1) most cases with persistent cognitive and emotional symptoms following mild head injury are based upon psychological and social considerations, including (although not particularly commonly) the effects of litigation, inconsistent and inadequate care (often a result of so-called "managed care"), family dynamics, the assumption of the role of "brain-damaged person," and a variety of other difficult to quantify considerations; and (2) a considerably smaller group persist in having cognitive and emotional deficits, as well as a variety of "neurologic" accompaniments of the injury, in the absence of clear-cut psychogenicity, which does suggest that many of these persons have a persistent biological deficit, more likely than not having to do with defective neurotransmitter functioning.

9780471184638 – FAST TRACK
Head Trauma Ca– Balem
0 – paperback